Ann-Mari Nilsson

THE
BIG 3
KNITTING
TECHNIQUES

How to Use Color, Slip Stitch,
and Relief Stitch Patterns to Create
Beautiful and Unique Garments

TRAFALGAR SQUARE
North Pomfret, Vermont

First published in the United States of America in 2018 by
Trafalgar Square Books
North Pomfret, Vermont 05053

Originally published in Swedish as *Sticka mönster*.

Copyright © 2017 Hemslöjdens förlag
English translation © 2018 Trafalgar Square Books

ISBN: 978-1-57076-903-0

Library of Congress Control Number: 2018945338

PATTERNS AND INSTRUCTIONS: Ann-Mari Nilsson
EDITOR: Cecilia Ljungström
PHOTOGRAPHY: Thomas Harrysson
DESIGN: Cecilia Ljungström
LAYOUT: Ulrika Rapp
COVER DESIGN: RM Didier
TRANSLATION INTO ENGLISH: Carol Huebscher Rhoades

Printed in China
10 9 8 7 6 5 4 3 2 1

Contents

Preface 5

READ THIS FIRST 7

SLIP-STITCH PATTERNS 11

Patterns 1-44 12

TWO-COLOR STRANDED KNITTING ... 57

Houndstooth 59
Golf 62
Forest 62
Aligned Stars 67
Diagonal Stars 68
Halland 72
Hälsing Fair 74

SURFACE TEXTURE PATTERNS 79

Patterns A–Y 80

BASIC GARMENT INSTRUCTIONS 105

Hat 106
Mittens 108
Pullover Vest 109
Buttoned Vest 114
Fine Little Sweater 120

Preface

Knitting patterns is absolutely one of my favorite things to do, and over the years I've designed many patterned garments. While working on this book, I dove deep into various techniques and came up with a selection of pattern motifs I hope you'll enjoy! The idea is that this book will function a little like a dictionary, where you can leaf back and forth and let yourself be inspired by various textures and options.

I've chosen three methods of patterning that range from easy to more difficult: surface patterns (also called relief or structure patterns), designs with slipped stitches, and two-color stranded knitting. The surface patterns produce the neatest and lightest knitting, while the stranded knitting is the strongest.

I've knitted up a lot of garments to demonstrate how the motifs can be used in various ways, and at the back of the book, you'll find basic instructions for these. But don't feel compelled to do exactly what I've done! You can combine motifs and knit completely different garments. Most of them can be done with all kinds of different methods, and there's no single right way to work a pattern of your own. Perhaps you already have too much yarn in your stash? Use it! Make new color choices, be inspired, and experiment. I'll only ask you to promise me two things: that you'll knit with wool yarn, and that you'll begin by reading the section with the heading "Read This First."

Thank you to Östergötlands Ullspinneri for all the yarn I used!
It's both fun and soothing to knit!
Ann-Mari Nilsson

READ THIS FIRST

PATTERN INSTRUCTIONS
Quickly read through the pattern instructions all the way to the end before you begin knitting so you have a general idea of the various steps involved. As you knit, read ahead into the next section carefully as you go; sometimes, steps worked simultaneously may be described over several sentences.

YARN
Don't worry too much about tracking down the exact same yarns I used. Work with wool yarns you have on hand or can get. The main information you need to verify is that the number of yards/meters per specified weight in your yarn matches that given in the pattern. Wool yarn with the number 1 = 1,000 m per kg = 100 m per 100 g. If the yarn description says 6/2, that means it's a two-ply yarn and each strand is 600 m per 100 g, which means the two strands plied together are 300 m per 100 g—this is between a fingering weight and sport weight, which is to say equivalent to CYCA #1-2 (super-fine to fine). In any patterns that use yarn of this weight doubled, you could also substitute a single strand of 6/4 or 3/2 yarn. Don't be afraid to try different yarns! You can always work a quick gauge swatch to test how a pattern stitch turns out with a particular yarn. It may not come out exactly like the photos in this book, but you might end up with a result you like even better.

You can also try www.yarnsub.com for suggestions. For more information on selecting or substituting yarn, contact your local yarn shop or an online store; they are familiar with all types of yarns and would be happy to help you. Additionally, the online knitting community at Ravelry.com has forums where you can post questions about specific yarns. Yarns come and go so quickly these days and there are so many beautiful yarns available.

If you don't have any suitable yarns in your stash already, a wide selection is available from:

Webs—America's Yarn Store
75 Service Center Road
Northampton, M A 01060
800-367-9327
www.yarn.com
customerservice@yarn.com

STITCH COUNT
When you are knitting, gauge (the stitch count in a specified number of inches or centimeters) is important! If you're working at a different gauge than that given in the

instructions, the garment will end up either too large or too small. Always knit a gauge swatch before you start the project and change to smaller or larger needles as needed.

SIZING

In this book, hats and mittens are sized for an "adult woman." The sizes for the vests are listed as XS (S, M, L, XL) where XS = a women's size 34 and XL = men's 56, approximately. We're all different, though! Measure and compare the given measurements with another garment that fits you well.

NEEDLES

It's often easier to knit back and forth on a circular needle than to use straight needles. When knitting with double-pointed needles (dpn), tighten the yarn when changing from needle to needle to avoid a ladder in the knitting.

CASTING ON

In my opinion, there's no reason not to cast on over two needles held together—it's so much easier.

EDGE STITCHES

Don't forget to knit edge stitches. By always knitting the first and last stitch of every row, an edge forms that will be easy to sew together when the garment is finished and easy to pick up and knit stitches through. Edge stitches are included in the patterns in this book unless otherwise specified.

STITCH COUNT

If the number of stitches in a pattern repeat you've chosen doesn't go evenly into the stitch count as given, you can just add or subtract a few stitches. You are working with a flexible material so it won't be noticeable. Just remember to write down what you've changed!

PATTERN FIT

When you are knitting patterned garments, you only need to measure the first section with a measuring tape. For the later sections, measure the pattern repeats instead. This way, the sections will be consistent in size and fit the patterning. Don't forget to center patterns—that means that the center of the pattern is placed at the center of the garment.

SPLICING

If you run out of one ball of yarn, you can splice the yarn from the next. Split the plies on both the old and new strands for a couple of inches / about 5 cm and overlap the strands. Gently spit on the overlapped strands and then rapidly roll the splice between your palms. Moisture, heat, and friction will felt the fibers to each other and make an invisible and strong join between the yarns.

INCREASING

There are several ways to increase stitches. One way is to use the needle tip to pick up the strand between two stitches and then knit into the back loop. This method is called a "make one," abbreviated as M1, and avoids a hole in the fabric.

SLIP STITCHES

To slip a stitch means to move a stitch from the left to right needle without knitting it. Slip the same way as the stitch would have been worked—either knitwise or purlwise.

THUMBHOLE

When knitting a mitten, you can make what I call an "afterthought" thumb by working the thumbhole stitches with smooth, contrast-color waste yarn, sliding those stitches back to the left needle, and knitting them again with the working yarn. If you are working a pattern with slipped stitches, you should place the thumbhole between two single-color rounds. If the pattern has slip stitches on all the rounds, just work the "thumb yarn" with the color for the round. When it's time to pick up and knit stitches around the thumbhole, insert one dpn into the stitches below the waste yarn and another dpn into the round above the waste yarn. Now carefully remove the waste yarn. Pick up and knit an extra stitch at each side of the hole and work it as a twisted stitch to avoid a hole. Sometimes, you might need to pick up and knit 2 or more stitches at the "corners" and then decrease them away on the following round(s).

GARMENT CARE

When your knitting is finished, it might feel a little hard and inelastic; maybe it stretches in the wrong direction, or the sizing is not completely perfect. Submerge it in lukewarm water, lightly spin it in the machine or gently squeeze (do not wring) out the extra water, or roll it in a hand towel and press out the water. Don't be afraid to pull slightly on the garment to make it fit better. Mittens can lay flat to dry. Wad a towel into hats to help shape them. Place the towel in a plastic bag that is somewhat smaller than the head size before you stuff it into the hat so the hat won't be stretched out. Lay the pieces for vests out on a flat surface to dry before you sew them up. Attach some of the yarn to sew the garment together with them.

WASHING

Don't wash unnecessarily! Air out the garment and wait to wash it until you see that it really is dirty. In that case, wash by hand, without any squeezing or wringing, using wool-safe soap and lukewarm water. Spin the garment lightly in a machine or roll it in a towel and press out the water. Lay the garment flat to dry.

DARNING

Keep an eye out for any signs of wear in your garments. It is easier to repair knitting before the holes appear. Use a strand of the yarn you knitted with and sew duplicate stitch over the worn stitches and the stitches around the worn area. Work with a blunt tapestry needle and follow the line of stitches.

SLIP-STITCH PATTERNS

SLIP-STITCH PATTERNS are worked with two or more colors, but only one color per row. On the row knitted with Color 1, slip the Color 2 stitches to the right needle without knitting them; on the row knitted with Color 2, slip the stitches of Color 1 to the right needle. It's easy and fun and the result looks much more complicated that it actually is. One color is always worked in an even number of stitches (on a right side (RS) row and on the wrong side (WS), if you are working back and forth). The technique works equally well back and forth or in the round. Try to knit with a light hand because the slipped stitches can stretch out and then the yarn you are knitting with will float too loosely on the wrong side of the fabric.

When you're working slip stitches, the piece will not be as sturdy as one worked with stranded knitting. Depending on which pattern you choose, the fabric might draw in a little, but you can fix that by soaking and blocking the knitting. The finished relief-stitch patterning will be so pretty!

CHART SYMBOLS—as seen on the right side (RS)

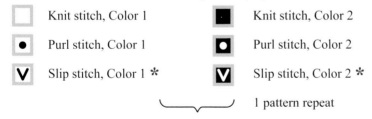

* Slip the stitch purlwise, with the yarn held behind if working on the RS and with the yarn in front if working on the WS. Slip the stitch to the right needle without working it.

The edge stitches are drawn on the charts to make the color changes obvious.

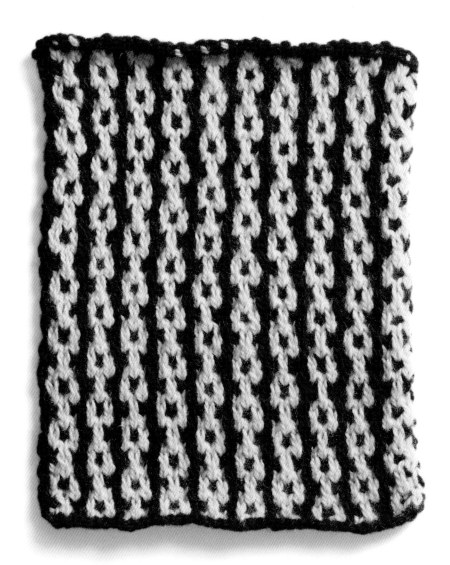

1

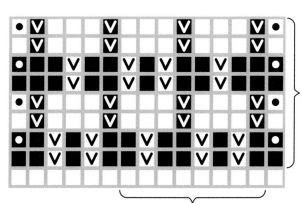

2

Work the repeat until the fabric is the desired width and length. This applies to all the charts in the book.

This vest is worked in Pattern 3.

3

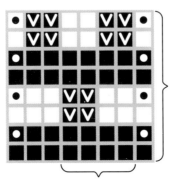

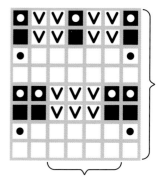

4

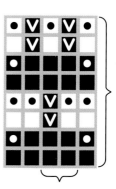

5

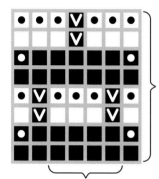

6

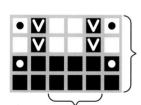

7

8

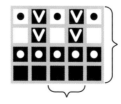

The front of the vest is worked in Pattern 8 and the back with Pattern 11.

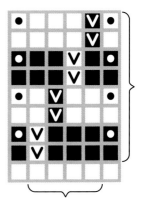

9

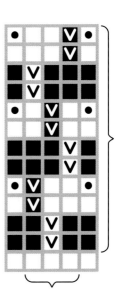

10

11

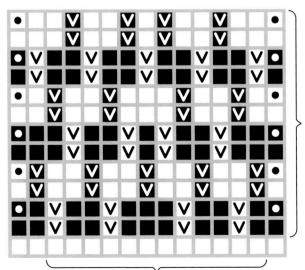

21

*The hat is knitted with
Pattern 12 and the
mittens in Pattern 9.*

12

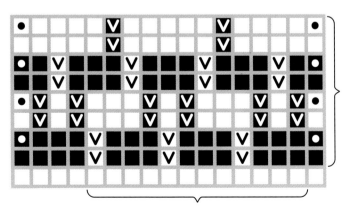

13

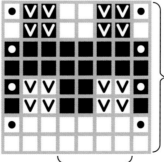

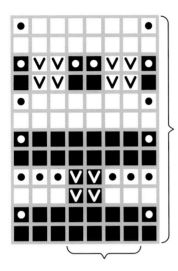

14

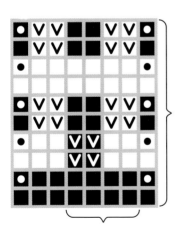

15

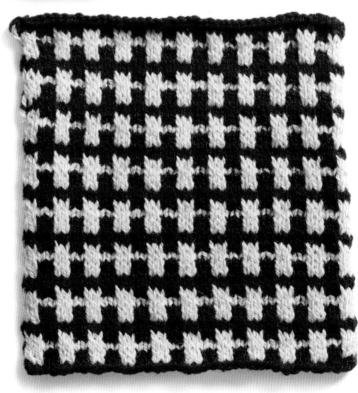

16

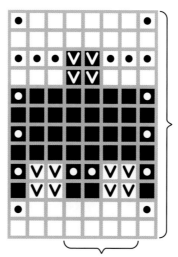

This pullover vest is worked in Pattern 12.

17

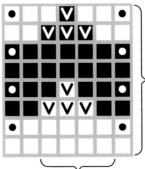

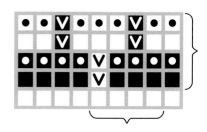

18

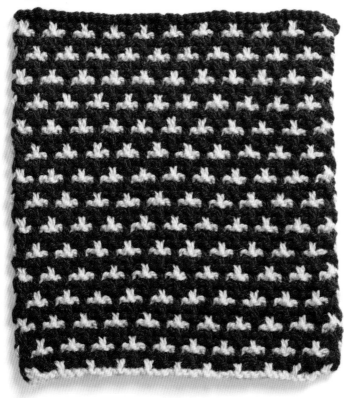

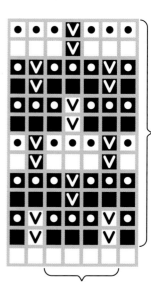

19

20

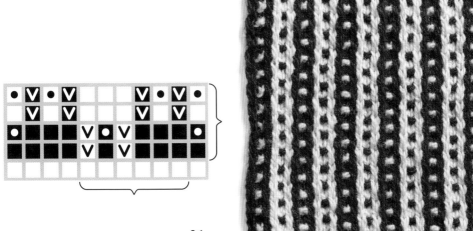

21

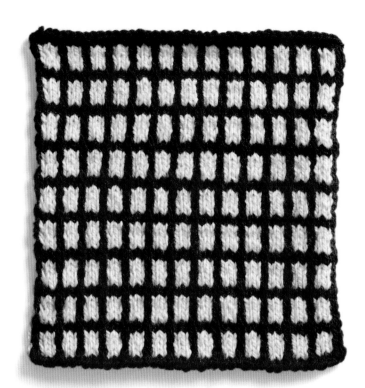

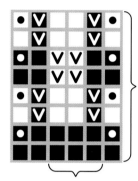

22

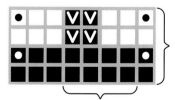

23

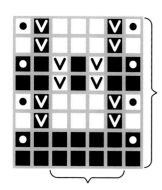

24

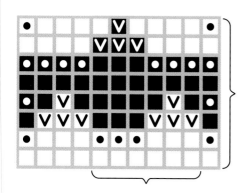

25

28

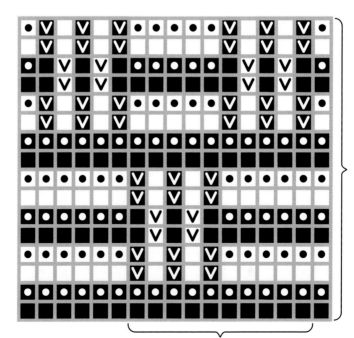

The pullover vest is worked in Pattern 28.

29

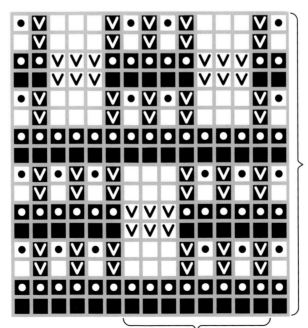

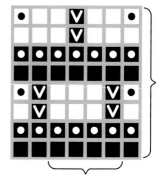

30

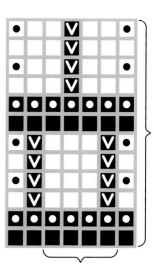

31

32

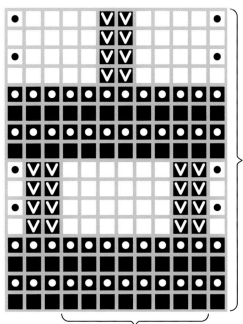

The hat is knitted in Pattern 33 while the mittens are worked in Pattern 31.

33

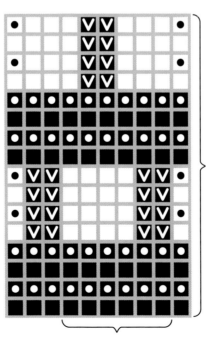

34

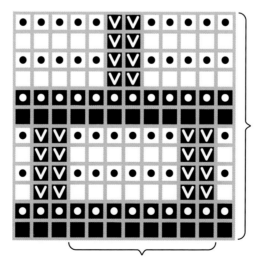

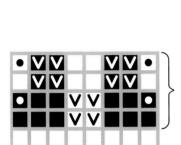

35

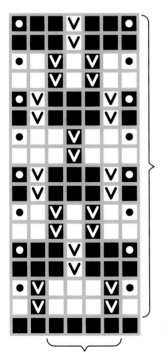

36

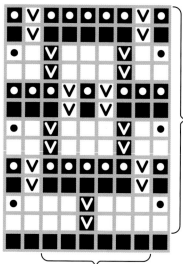

37

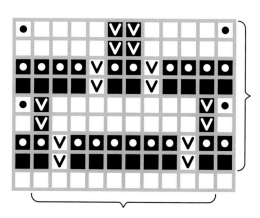

38

39

40

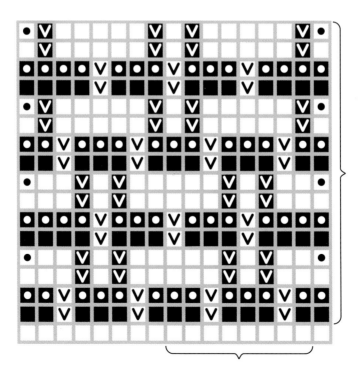

41

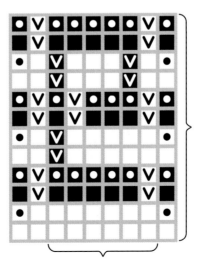

42

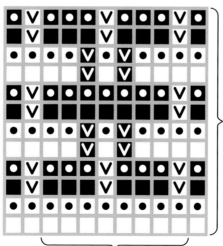

43

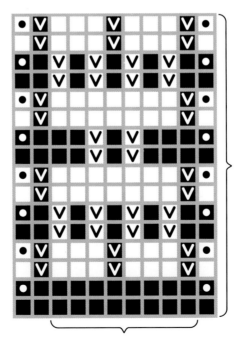

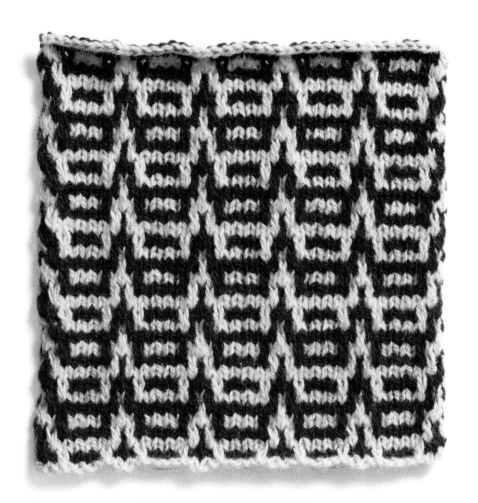

44

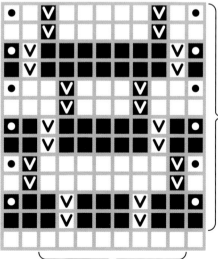

These mittens are knitted with Pattern 31. On the page opposite, you'll find Houndstooth pattern mittens. The front of the vest is worked in Pattern 8 and back with Pattern 11.

TWO-COLOR STRANDED KNITTING

CLASSIC TWO-COLOR STRANDED KNITTING produces the warmest and sturdiest garments. It's worked in stockinette stitch with two strands of yarn in different colors that run parallel as you work. If there are long color sections (color floats) in the design, you have to twist the two yarns around each other on the back (wrong side) of the fabric at least every third stitch, or sometimes every other stitch (if the twists can't occur evenly), to catch the yarn not in use. To keep the twists from showing on the right side, it's important not to twist the yarns at the same place on the following row/round. Stretch the knitting when it comes to the right needle so it doesn't draw in. Knit with both yarns together in the edge stitches.

For this section, I've collected a few classic and useful patterns. Most are easy to learn and do not have long floats.

CHART SYMBOLS—as seen on the right side

☐ Color 1

■ Color 2

⌣ 1 pattern repeat

The edge stitches are *not* included on the charts.

Houndstooth

This pattern is unbelievably easy to knit, and has a complex "tweedy" look. This is one of my absolute favorite patterns, and I've made many pairs of mittens in different color combinations with it. Try this one out in colors that are "tone on tone!"

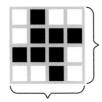

Vest and swatch strip in Houndstooth pattern.

Hat in the Golf pattern with
Houndstooth mittens.
On the page opposite, a
Golf-patterned vest.

Golf

Golf is an easily-knitted variation of a very classic pattern. It's usually seen on the front of a sweater or vest but works just as well on a hat or pair of mittens.

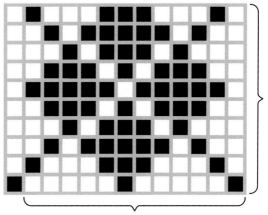

Forest

The spruce pattern has become a whole forest! As I knitted the mittens shown on page 65, I thought of a forest against a clear blue sky and snow on the ground. On the hat, the moon has risen over the forest and glistens in the water.

In some places, the color changes are a little far apart, so don't forget to twist the strands around each other often!

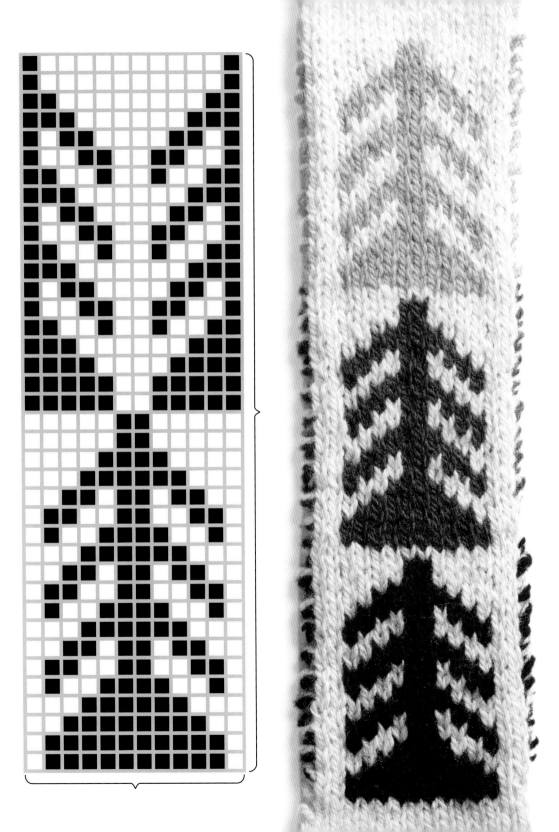

Hat and mittens combining the Forest pattern with the Hälsing Fair blocks. A Forest design covers the vest on the page opposite.

Aligned Stars

Here's the traditional star motif in its simplest form with close color changes. The pattern's quite easy to memorize. Here I've chosen to knit the stars in a color against a white background, but it looks just as striking with white stars against a colored background.

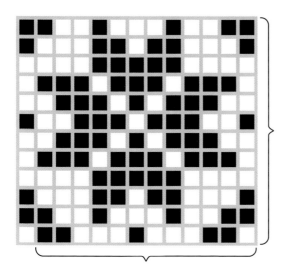

Vest and swatch strip in the Aligned Stars pattern.

Diagonal Stars

The stars in this overall pattern are identical to those in the Aligned Stars pattern on page 67, but they are arranged diagonally. The repeat is larger, so it'll take a little more time to memorize the pattern sequence. You can also combine both star patterns.

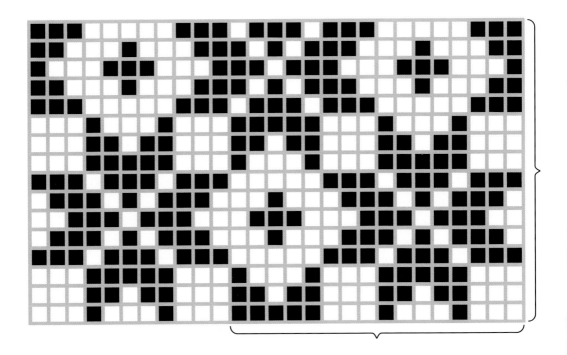

On opposing page, a vest in the Diagonal Stars pattern.

On the page opposite, a
hat with the Diagonal
Stars pattern and mittens
with Aligned Stars.

Hat and mittens in the
Halland pattern.

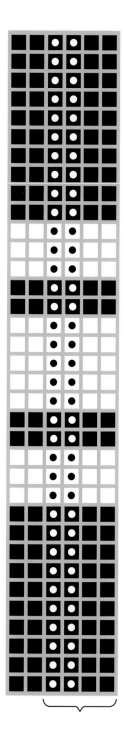

Halland

You'll find this pattern on fishermen's sweaters from Halland, a province on the southwest coast of Sweden. If you like, you can use the panel separately. The second motif is very practical because the repeat is so small.

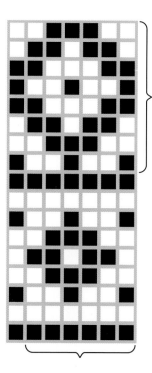

Opposite page—knitted fabric with the Halland motif.

Hälsing Fair

Hälsing Fair is a medley of motifs from traditional sweaters from Hälsingland (a province in central Sweden). Combine the motifs and colors as you like. If you have a stash of leftover yarns at home, they'll be quite useful for these patterns. When you're knitting the blocks at the bottom of the first chart, let the strands float freely on the back so the squares will bow out a little.

Hat and mittens in the Hälsing Fair pattern. On the opposite page, a close-up of a cardigan with the same pattern.

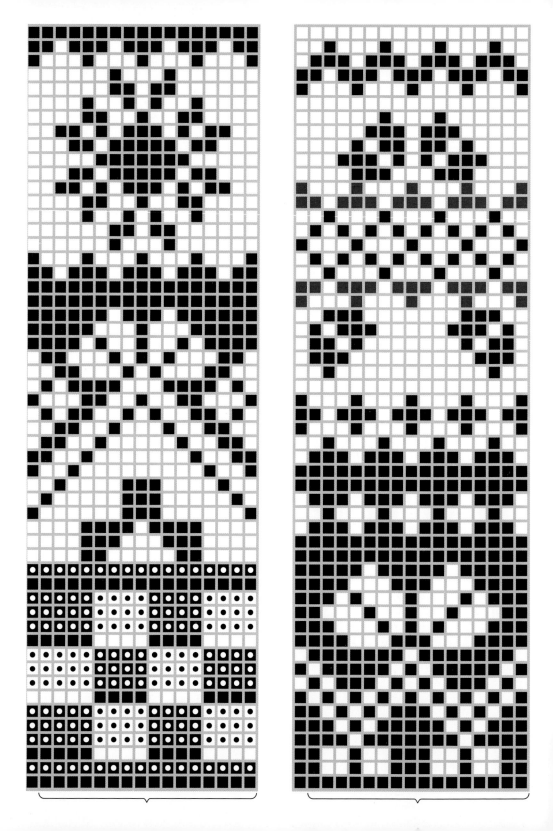

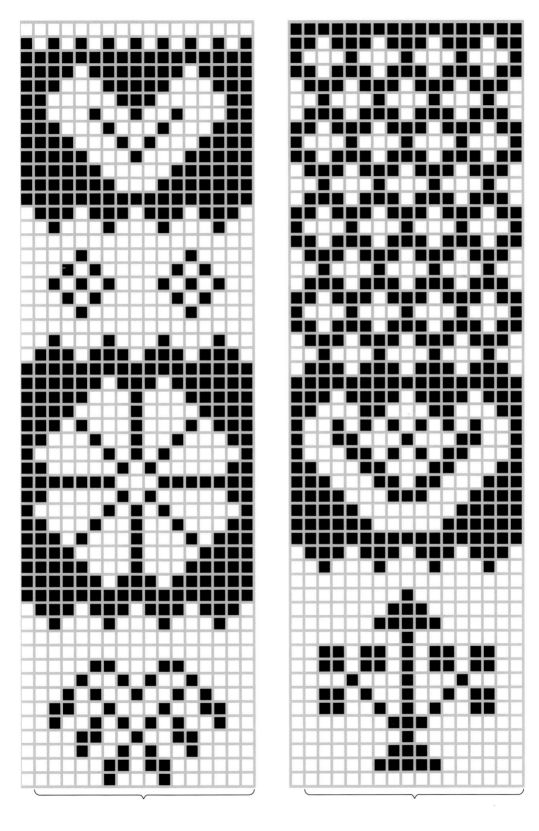

RELIEF STITCH PATTERNS

RELIEF STITCH PATTERNS produce a fine and supple garment. They consist of knit and purl stitches in a single color. Knit firmly so the pattern is clearly visible. When the pattern is worked, it doesn't look anything like the chart—something unexpected happens when a purl stitch is placed right next to a knit stitch. When knitting relief stitch patterns, the fabric might draw in, but it will assume its proper look after you've soaked and blocked it.

CHART SYMBOLS—as seen on the right side (RS)

☐   Knit stitch

▣   Purl stitch

The entire chart corresponds to one repeat and is repeated in its entirety. The edge stitches are *not* included on the charts.

A pullover vest knitted in Pattern A.

A

81

B

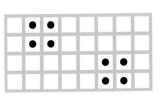

C

D

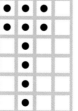

E

Buttoned vest in Pattern E.

F

	●			●	●	
	●		●	●	●	
		●	●		●	
	●	●	●		●	
	●	●			●	
	●				●	

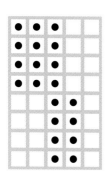

G

H

Pullover vest worked in Pattern I.

I

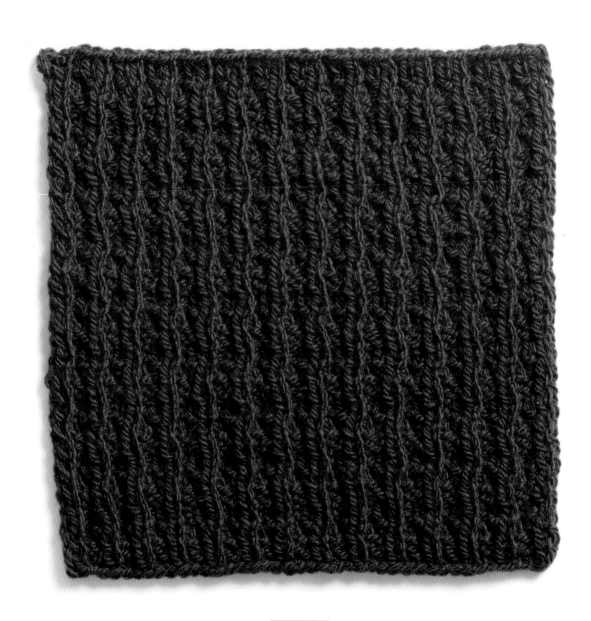

J

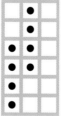

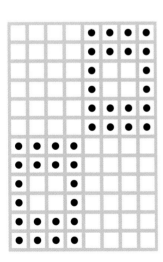

K

L

This hat features Pattern M and the mittens Pattern N.

M

N

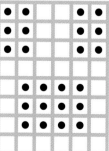

O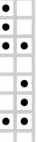

P

Pattern P is used for this buttoned vest.

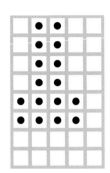

Q

R

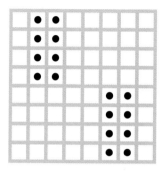

S

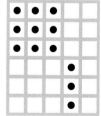

T

*A hat with Pattern Q and
mittens with Pattern U.*

U

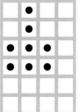

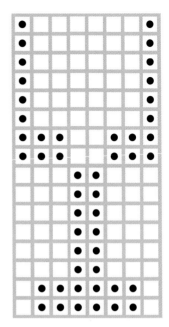

V

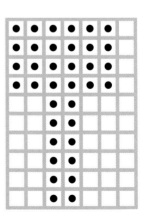

X

Y

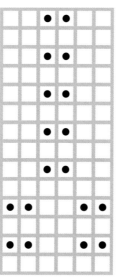

103

BASIC GARMENT INSTRUCTIONS

ABBREVIATIONS

BO	bind off (= British cast off)	rem(s)(ing)	remain(s)(ing)
cm	centimeter(s)	rnd(s)	round(s)
CO	cast on	p	purl
dpn	double-pointed needles	pm	place marker
in	inch(es)	RS	right side
k	knit	ssk	slip, slip, knit = (sl 1 knitwise) 2 times, knit the 2 sts together through back loops = left-leaning decrease, 1 st decreased
k2tog	knit 2 together = right-leaning decrease; 1 stitch decreased		
M1	make 1 = lift strand between 2 stitches and knit into back loop = 1 stitch increased	st(s)	stitch(es)
		tbl	through back loop(s)
mm	millimeter(s)	WS	wrong side

The red and black mitten on the opposite page is knitted in Pattern 9 while the red and white mitten features Aligned Stars. The vest is worked with Pattern I.

Yarn Amounts: 250 (250, 300, 350, 350) g

Needles: U. S. sizes 1.5 and 2.5 / 2.5 and 3 mm: 32 in / 80 cm circulars

GAUGE
26 sts in pattern on larger needles = 4 in / 10 cm.
Adjust needle sizes to obtain correct gauge if necessary.

BACK
With smaller circular, CO 102 (112, 122, 132, 142) sts. Work back and forth in k1, p1 ribbing for 2½ (2½, 2½, 2¾, 2¾) in / 6 (6, 6, 7, 7) cm.

Change to larger circular and pattern. On the first row, increase 10 sts evenly spaced across = 112 (122, 132, 142, 152) sts. Continue in pattern until piece measures 9½ (9¾, 10¾, 11½, 12 ¾) in / 24 (25, 27, 29, 32) cm.

Shape armholes: At each side, BO 5 (6, 6, 7, 7) sts. Now decrease on every other row 3-2-2-2-1-1-1 sts and then, on every 4th row, 1-1 sts = 74 (82, 92, 100, 110) sts rem.
Continue without further shaping until armhole depth is 8 (8¾, 9½, 10¼, 11) in / 20 (22, 24, 26, 28) cm and the total length is now 19¾ (21, 22½, 24½, 26½) in / 50 (53, 57, 62, 67) cm.

Neck and shoulder shaping: BO the center 28 (30, 32, 34, 36) sts = 23 (26, 30, 33, 37) sts rem for each side. Work each side separately.

At beginning of every neck edge row, BO 2-2-2 sts and, *at the same time*, shape shoulder: At beginning of every shoulder edge row, BO 5-6-6 (6-7-7; 8-8-8; 9-9-9; 10-10-11) sts. Work the other side to correspond, reversing shaping to match.

FRONT
Work as for back until piece measures 16½ (17¼, 18½, 20, 21¾) in / 42 (44, 47, 51, 55) cm.

NOTE: If you are working a V-neck, CO 1 st at center.

Round neck: BO the center 12 (14, 16, 18, 20) sts and work each side separately = 31 (34, 38, 41, 45) sts rem. At neck edge, BO 4-3-2-1-1-1-1-1 sts = 17 (20, 24, 27, 31) sts rem. Continue without further shaping until armhole depth is same as on back to shoulder. Shape shoulder as for back. Work the other side to correspond, reversing shaping to match.

V-neck: When front measures 14¼ (15, 16¼, 17¾, 19¼) in / 36 (38, 41, 45, 49) cm, place the center st on a holder. Work each side separately. At neck edge, decrease 1 st on every other row 20 (21, 22, 23, 24) times = 17 (20, 24, 27, 31) sts rem. Continue without further shaping until armhole depth is same as on back. Shape shoulder as for back. Work the other side to correspond, reversing shaping to match.

FINISHING
Soak garment in lukewarm water and lightly squeeze out excess water. Pat out pieces to finished measurements on a flat surface with an absorbent towel underneath or on blocking mat; let dry completely. Seam one shoulder.

In this pattern, all ribbed bands are worked back and forth.

Round neck: With smaller circular, pick up and knit 116 (124, 132, 140, 148) sts around neck. Work back and forth in k1, p1 ribbing for ¾ in / 2 cm. BO in ribbing. Seam other shoulder.

V-neck: With smaller circular, pick up and knit 143 (155, 167, 179, 191) sts around neck, including the st at center front. Keeping the center front st as a knit st on RS, purl on WS, work back and forth in k1, p1 ribbing and shape as follows:

On every other row, decrease 2 sts at center front with a centered double decrease: slip 2 sts knitwise at the same time, k1, psso.

BO in ribbing when band is ¾ in / 2 cm. Seam other shoulder.

Armhole bands: With smaller circular, pick up and knit approx. 130 (140, 150, 160, 170) sts. Work back and forth in k1, p1 ribbing for ¾ in / 2 cm. BO in ribbing. Seam sides.

Soak garment in lukewarm water and lightly squeeze out excess water. Pat out to finished measurements on a flat surface with an absorbent towel underneath or on blocking mats; let dry completely.

Weave in all ends neatly on WS.

Button band: With smaller circular, pick up and knit approx. 121 (127, 135, 145, 155) sts along the front edge of the side with buttons and work back and forth in k1, p1 ribbing for ¾ in / 2 cm. BO in ribbing.

Mark the spacing for the buttons with approx. 2¾ in / 7 cm between each button. Count the garter ridges to help space the buttons evenly.

Make the other front the same way with the buttonholes over 3 sts or ¼ in / 0.75 cm.

Count the garter ridges to help space the buttonholes evenly.

Multi-color vest, V-neck with button band: With an extra-long, smaller circular, pick up and knit approx. 339 (359, 383, 411, 439) sts around the front edges, V-neck and back neck. Work back and forth in k1, p1 ribbing for ¼ in / 0.75 cm.

Measure for the placement of the buttonholes with approx. 2¾ in / 7 cm between each buttonhole. Count the garter ridges to help space the buttonholes evenly and to match placement of buttons. Make each buttonhole over 3 sts.

When band measures ¾ in / 2 cm, BO in ribbing.

All vests, armhole bands: With smaller circular, pick up and knit approx. 130 (140, 150, 160, 170) sts around armhole. Work around in k1, p1 ribbing for ¾ in / 2 cm. BO in ribbing.

Seam sides.

Soak garment in lukewarm water and lightly squeeze out excess water. Lay vest on a towel on a flat surface and pat out to finished measurements. Leave until completely dry. Weave in all ends neatly on WS. Sew on buttons.

The mittens on the opposite page are worked with the Halland pattern while the vest is knitted in Pattern P.

A Fine Little Cardigan

This cardigan must be knitted in the round and cut open—but it's not that dangerous, I promise. You can knit it in any pattern you like! The finishing takes some time but it's totally worth it. This might not be the best choice, though, if you haven't knitted before.

The design is close-fitting and short. Measure a garment you already have to determine the right size. The instructions are for sizes 34-42 (approximately). If you don't want to have hooks and clasps, you can sew in a separating zipper instead.

LEVEL OF DIFFICULTY
Advanced

SIZE
XS (S, M)

FINISHED MEASUREMENTS
Chest: 34 (36¼, 38½) in / 86 (92, 98) cm
Length, as measured down center back: 19¼ (20, 21) in / 49 (51, 53) cm

MATERIALS
Yarn:
CYCA # (sport/baby), 6/2 100% wool yarn (328 yd/300 m / 100 g)
Yarn Amounts: total of 450 (500, 600) g

Notions: 8 pairs of large hooks and eyes (see page 125) or separating zipper, length to fit down center front when finished.

Needles: U. S. size 2.5 / 3 mm: 32 in / 80 cm circular and set of 5 dpn

GAUGE
27 sts in pattern = 4 in / 10 cm.
Adjust needle size to obtain correct gauge if necessary.

Fine Little Cardigan in the Hälsing Fair design.

*A cardigan knitted in the round
with steeks up the center front
and armholes.*

FINE LITTLE CARDIGAN IN HÄLSING FAIR PATTERN

BODY
With circular, CO 234 (250, 266) sts; join, being careful not to twist cast-on row. Knit 1 rnd. On Rnd 2, knit the first 9 sts for the steek (a steek is a set of extra sts that will be reinforced and cut open later). On Rnd 3, begin working the 9 steek sts in vertical stripes = alternate knitting 1 color and then another. Work rem sts in pattern.

Work in pattern following the charts on pages 76-77 for about 11¾ in / 30 cm.

Now, knit 55 (59, 63) sts, BO 16 sts for armhole, knit 101 (109, 117) sts, BO 16 sts, knit 46 (50, 54) sts.

On the next rnd, knit to the armhole, CO 9 sts for the steek, knit to opposite armhole, CO 9 sts for steek, and complete rnd.

Knit 1 rnd.

Shape armhole: At armhole edge, on each side of the 9-st steek at each side, decrease 1 st on every rnd 4 times and then 1 st on every other rnd 4 times. When armhole measures 3¼ (3½, 4) in / 8 (9, 10) cm, shape neck by binding off the first 25 sts (= steek + 16) sts and the last 16 sts of rnd.
CO 9 sts for a steek over the bound-off sts at neck. Continue in pattern until armhole depth is 8¼ (9, 9¾) in / 21 (23, 25) cm. BO.

SLEEVES
With dpn, CO 56 sts (all sizes). Divide sts onto 4 dpn; join and pm for beginning of rnd. Center the pattern. Work 5 tiers of blocks if your arms are long; otherwise, work 3 tiers of blocks as on the body.

Size M: On the first rnd after the blocks, increase 10 sts evenly spaced around = 66 sts.
All sizes: Increase 1 st on each side of the last st of the rnd on every 7th rnd 17 (20, 20) times = 90 (96, 106) sts.

When sleeve is desired length to underarm, BO 7 sts at the beginning of the rnd and 8 sts at the end. CO 9 sts for a steek.

Shape sleeve cap: On each side of the steek, decrease 1 st on every rnd 4 times, 1 st on every other rnd 17 (20, 23) times, and then 1 st on every rnd 10 times = 13 (13, 17) sts + 9 steek sts rem. BO rem sts.

FINISHING

To reinforce steeks at center front and on armholes, machine-stitch 2 lines on each side of the center st of steek. With sharp scissors, carefully cut steek open along center stitch.

Reinforce and cut open sleeve cap steeks and then reinforce the cut edges by machine-stitching straight lines across edges.

Pin shoulders, slanting them down gradually about ¾ in / 2 cm for shaping (see photo on page 125); baste. Seam shoulders just below basting line.

Turn the edge of the back neck down ¾ in / 2 cm, sloping the turned edge down towards the shoulder. Sew down folded edges on WS.

Attach sleeves. Fold the armhole cut edges under and sew them down. Turn the neck cut edges under and sew them down.

Pick up 21 sts around lower edge of neck on one side and work in stockinette for ⅜ in / 1 cm.

Purl 1 row on RS (foldline). Continue working in stockinette for ⅜ in / 1 cm after the foldline and then BO. Turn the edge under and sew down on inside. Do the same on the other side.

Pick up and knit 105 (108, 111) sts along one front edge and work back and forth in stockinette for ¾ in / 2 cm. Purl 1 row on RS for foldline. Continue in stockinette for ¾ in / 2 cm for facing and then BO.

Do the same on the opposite front edge.

Turn the front edges at the foldline and sew down on WS. Weave in all ends neatly on WS.

The opposite page shows the inside of the cardigan
with all the finishing details.

Soak the sweater in lukewarm water and then gently squeeze out excess water. Lay the sweater on a towel over a flat surface and pat out to finished measurements. You can shape the sleeves by stuffing each with a terry cloth towel.

On the WS, sew on 8 pairs of hooks and eyes evenly spaced down the front, or sew in a separating zipper.

Pattern Notes

Pattern Notes

Pattern Notes